KINGFISHER
LONDON & NEW YORK

First edition published 1994 by Kingfisher
This edition published 2017 by Kingfisher
Published in the United States by Kingfisher,
175 Fifth Ave., New York, NY 10010
Kingfisher is an imprint of Macmillan Children's Books, London.
All rights reserved.

Copyright © Alan Baker 1994

Distributed in the U.S. and Canada by Macmillan,
175 Fifth Ave., New York, NY 10010

Library of Congress Cataloging-in-Publication data
has been applied for.

ISBN: 978-0-7534-7322-1 (HB)
ISBN: 978-0-7534-7323-8 (PB)

Kingfisher books are available for special promotions
and premiums. For details contact: Special Markets
Department, Macmillan, 175 Fifth Ave.,
New York, NY 10010.

For more information, please visit
www.kingfisherbooks.com

Printed in China
9 8 7 6 5 4 3 2 1
1TR/1116/WKT/UG/157MA

Aa

A is for apple.

BLACK AND WHITE RABBIT'S
ABC

LITTLE RABBITS

ALAN BAKER

KINGFISHER
NEW YORK

Bb

B is for box,
where Rabbit
puts the apple.

Cc

C is for crayon,
held in Rabbit's paw.

Dd

D is for drawing.

Ee

E is for easel,
to rest Rabbit's
drawing on.

Ff

F is for falling
as the apple
topples over.

Gg

G is for glue,
icky-sticky
glue.

Hh

H is for hopping,
with a sticky paw.

Ii

I is for ink bottle,
right in Rabbit's way.

Jj

J is for jumping,
but not high enough!

Kk

K is for
kicking
it over.
Whoops!

Ll

L is for leaking
all over the floor.

Mm

M is the mess,
soon mopped up.

Nn

N is for nose,
covered in ink.

Oo

O is for
opening
a new jar
of paint.

Pp

P is for the paint,

a bright apple green.

Qq

Q is for
quick!
Paint
in the
picture.

Rr

R is for runny, the paint's not thick enough.

Ss

S is for spilling as paint drips off the brush.

Tt

T is for turning.

Uu

U is for
upside down.

Vv

V is for very good.
Rabbit's painting
is done.

Ww

W is for water
to wash
the brushes.

Xx

X is for the kisses
that Rabbit
draws on his
painting.

Yy

Y is for
yawning.
What
a hard
day's
work!

Zz

Z is for zzzzzzzzz.
Rabbit's fast asleep.

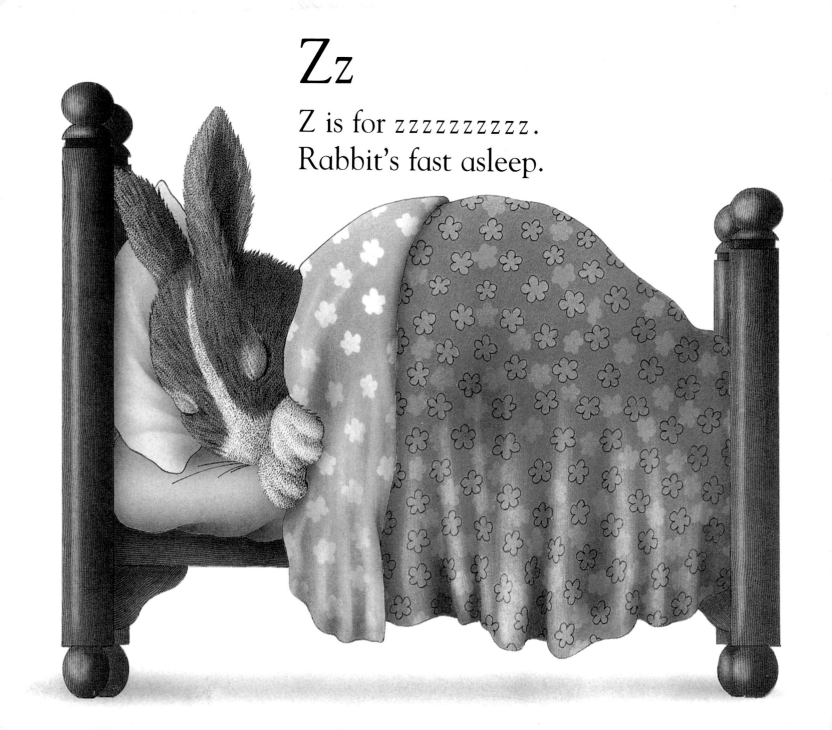